WE SEEK ASYLUM

Gustavo Adolfo Aybar

Willow Books
Detroit, Michigan

We Seek Asylum

Editors: Randall Horton & Monica Prince
Cover art by Larry Thomas

ISBN 978-0-9992232-2-2

LCCN 2017959213

Willow Books, a Division of Aquarius Press
www.WillowLit.net

Acknowledgments

"Baseball's Travelin' Men: In Praise of the Latin and Negro Leagues"
- *Somos en Escrito* Online Journal. Aug. 26, 2014.
- *KCPT: Arts Upload Season 2, Episode 1.* Air date Sep. 25, 2014.
- Forthcoming in *Afro-Latino Poetry Anthology.* Edited by Melissa Castillo-Garsow. Forthcoming by Arte Publico Press.

"Morir Soñando"
- *Many Windows*, Magnapoets Anthology Series 4 *Epiphanies Anthology* and *¡Manteca! An Anthology of Afro-Latino Poets.* Edited by Melissa Castillo-Garsow. Arte Publico Press.

"The Only Thing I Have"
- *Collecting Life: Poets on Objects Known and Imagined.* Edited by Madelyn Garner and Andrea L. Watson. 3: A Taos Press, 2013.
- *Whistling Fire.* Mar 27, 2012.
- *Tuesday Poet.* theblackbottom.com. Aug 16, 2011.

"Tia Licha's House"
- "Tia Licha's House." *Number One.* University of Missouri-Kansas City. Vol. 59, 2006.

Printed in the United States of America

To my mother, Virginia Antonia and my son, Bécquer Francisco.

I hope you trust and are proud of the men we are and of the men we are
yet to become.
—¡Los quiero un montón de montones!

Contents

III.

PROLOGUE

"[Baseball] is about time and timelessness, speed and grace, failure and loss, imperishable hope, and coming home."

—Ken Burns

"I should like to be able to love my country and still love justice."
— Albert Camus

Remembering the Dead

We have these pictures you see—his legend. You have his laugh.
Grandpa Satch played with flair from sandlots to big league stadiums;
he'd arrive and *it was like the sun coming from behind a cloud.*
This season on the island, Uncle Josh, the Trujillo Dragons,
there aren't any people alive who were there to tell it.
Oh, the homers, the pitches, the freedom, the fear:
they were All-Stars, I say.
As we move along the Negro Leagues Museum,
I tell my son stories. Of your lore
I speak, your name and claim. You kin?

I speak your name and claim you kin;
I tell my son stories of your lore
as we move along the Negro Leagues Museum.
They were all stars, I say.
Oh, the homers, the pitches, the freedom, the fear.
There aren't any people alive who were there. To tell it:
this season on the island, Uncle Josh, the Trujillo Dragons.
He'd arrive and *it was like the sun coming from behind a cloud—*
Grandpa Satch; played with flair, from sandlots to big league stadiums.
We have these pictures; you see his legend. You have his laugh.

I.

Corpse Disposal

The countless decomposing cadavers left their scent unanchored
along every street in Santo Domingo; the air akin to rotten fish and sulphur.

Hurricane season reminds us of our undeveloped instinct to flee
to high ground, to detect changes in air pressure or the movement of sound

and worm or bird our way to safer surroundings.
The San Zenon's roar rose from a green storm-tossed sea

and a butterfly's wings remained soft and folded against its body.
How many people knew Trujillo's reign came disguised as light wind?

How many ignored the warnings through his development and decay,
complicit in the slaughter of reported hurricane victims and others to come?

Next year at this time the city shall be rebuilt and renamed Ciudad Trujillo,
while the forecast remained unable to predict the island's

decades-long struggle with this tree-tossing beast
and the lives he took along his path.

Baseball's Travelin' Men: In Praise of the Latin and Negro Leagues
After Martín Espada's poem, "Alabanza"

Alabanza. Praise the ballplayers with their call and response
and scars on their bodies that said Oye,
black athletes with ties to the Negro Leagues,
the sole option for play decades ago.
Praise the talent in the Negro Leagues: men
black as the bottom of the sea, to a honey gold.
Alabanza. Praise the Kansas City-Paseo YMCA
where Rube Foster and others birthed the teams,
plucked dirt from the gutter, refined it to cleanliness.
Alabanza. Shall we praise Gus Greenle, his numbers racket and Pittsburgh,
for providing a place where only the ball was white?
So that every action meant a hurling, a casting out,
a slamming away and dismantling the institution, sanctifying
blackness. Praise the blackness. *Alabanza.*

Praise Quisqueya's shine from across the Atlantic Ocean,
like gold glimpsed through the eyes of ancient conquistadors.
Praise the conquistadors, the island's Tainos, its fruit, its soil.
Alabanza. Praise the brutality of Rafael Leonidas Trujillo Molina (Chapitas)
taking Greenle's ballclub and putting it in Santo Domingo.
Praise the broken contracts, luggage filled with cash, Satchel Paige
and Cool Papa, Josh Gibson and Sammy Bankhead, Cy Perkins and the others
arriving on biplanes, landing on the Rio Higuamo,
right in front of the main church.
Alabanza. Praise Trujillo's friends, enforcers of the national image
and their leader's prestige: murdering civilians
who opposed him—inserting politics into a sport developing its purity.

Alabanza. Praise the scout under Trujillo's orders who conspired to defraud the
Crawfords of Satchel Paige and got arrested twice during his pursuit. *Alabanza.*

After the applause wilder than applause,
after Satchel and the team understood
that anything bearing Trujillo's name will not lose,
after he unveiled the secrets of a thousand pitches: the trouble ball,
the triple curve, the whipsy-dipsy-do, a swing, a miss.
After military forces clobbered those against Ciudad Trujillo,
after the near loss of three games to none,

and the winning of the pennant by Ciudad Trujillo,
for a time the Latin and Negro Leagues shined
with the greatest players to ever play,
like the conquistadors' gold. Gold I say, even if the fans cannot tell us
about the gray in Trujillo's mustache, shaved at the edges,
except the three to five centimeter above the centre of the lip.
Because he had no lips.
Gold I say, to name the fastballs flung in revolutions
across the mound of this stadium and stadiums to come.
Alabanza I say, even if Trujillo had no lips.

Alabanza. When the leagues began, from America, Latin America,
México and the Caribbean Basin,
revolutions of fastballs rose and drifted towards each other,
lightning-crowned, and one said with a Spanish tongue:
let me play; we have no field here.
And the other said with an African tongue,
I will let you play. Baseball is all we have.

Corvus

Once,
my
mother
told me how
Dominican streets
quieted to the sounds of
the national anthem sung over the radio;
each proud citizen rendered honors; their cry
like caws, resembled a murder of crows.

Early Dominicanization Campaigns

PORT AU PRINCE, Haiti, Oct. 24— ███████████
███ more than 500 persons ███ killed ███████████ along
the Haitian-Dominican frontier. ██████████
█████████ Haitians.

███████████████████ persons who escaped
█████████ predicted ███████████ 1,700 dead ███
wounded, mostly women and children.

███████████████████████
██████████ Dominican Republic against heavy immigration of Haitian
laborers. ███ government ████████████
███████████████████████

█████████████████ will not tolerate ██████
███ any threat to their security.

███████████████████████ 1936 ██████
█████ agreement ████████████
███████████████████████

What the Yankis Left Behind

Before it was more than a game,
before a player ever became a prophet,
or stadium visits turned events, turned treks,
turned pilgrimages, San Pedro sugar mill workers
played U.S. marines for fun, and along
with an increased fervor for the sport,
left as its most telling legacy, Trujillo.

The Rise of a Dictator: Rafael Leonidas Trujillo Molina (Chapitas)

Born October 24, 1891, San Cristobal, Dominican Republic, later known as "Bethlehem."

Nearly dies from diphtheria at age seven; (see: inauguration of Dr. Miguel Brioso Bustillos Hospital); (see: penitential rite).

Nicknamed "Chapitas," slang for the bottle caps he collected like bodies; (see: how to abolish a word from a people's vocabulary); (see: rope); (see: bullet).

1913: At twenty-two works as a security guard for a sugar company and as a telegraph operator. Serves jail time for theft, then again for forgery.

1919: Enters Dominican Constabulary as a Lieutenant.

1921: Becomes Second Lieutenant.

July 12, 1924: The American flag comes down over Fort Ozama, ends the eight-year Marine occupation. The republic returns to native hands.

1924-1926: Promoted to Captain then Lieutenant Colonel.

Trujillo speaks to a Lieutenant Sanabia, reveals to the officer his wife's infidelity and the name of her lover. The Lieutenant kills a Major Lora and Mrs. Sanabia.
(Enter Major Trujillo).

1928: Becomes Chief of Staff Brigadier General of the National Army.

August, 1930: At thirty-nine years of age, Trujillo assumes office of the presidency of the Dominican Republic.

September 3, 1930: The San Zenon Hurricane destroys Santo Domingo: over 2,000 dead, over 8,000 injured. The capital city is later rebuilt & renamed Ciudad Trujillo.

1935: Marries ex-mistress and third wife, María de los Angeles Martínez Alba. She gives birth to three of his children: Rafael L. (Ramfis) Trujillo, Jr.; Maria de los Angeles del Corazon de Jesus (Angelita); Leonidas Rhadames Trujillo.

1935: Suffers from chronic prostate affliction; Dr. George Marion saves his life; (see: penitential rite).

Summer 1937: The acquisition of many professional Negro League baseball players like Satchel Paige, "Cool Papa" Bell, and many others, led to Trujillo creating one of the greatest teams ever assembled in the history of the sport. The season was so costly that professional baseball on the island did not resume again until 1951.

October 2, 1937: The Cutting; (see: sprig of parsley); (see: Articulatory Difficulties in the Acquisition of Spanish /r/); (see: Haitian genocide).

1939: World War II begins.

1940: Dr. Dario Contreras performs a daring operation to remove anthrax in Trujillo's neck. (Again, see: penitential rite).

1941: The Dominican Republic declares war on axis powers: Japan, Germany, and Italy.

1947: Trujillo declares bombs would fall on Havana the moment the first invader steps on his island; calls off the Cayo Confites military plot, which originated in Cuba and consisted of 1000 men.

June 14, 1959: Dominican exiles from Cuba are defeated during another attempt to assassinate Trujillo. The attacks on the cities of Estero Hondo, Maimon, and Constanza spawn the new revolutionary group Catorce de Junio Movimiento.

1960: Assassination plot for the 21st of January is thwarted a day before by the secret police; (see: La Cuarenta Prison); (see: mock executions); (see: cattle prod).

November 19, 1960: Patria, Minerva, and Maria Teresa Mirabal are brutally beaten with clubs and choked to death. With the cadavers inside the sisters' Land Rover, the vehicle is pushed over a precipice, tires trampling the silence along the route that connects Calle Luperón and Carretera Duarte, on the margins of the Guazumal River. (see: *The Tipping Point*); (see: Julia Alvarez); (see: *In the Time of Butterflies*).

May 30, 1961: Trujillo's car is ambushed on a road outside the capital; his last breath finds him bullet filled, sprawled across the highway, several feet away from his Chevy Packard. Ramfis returns from Paris to capture, torture and execute the assassins, then flees to France months after with his father's casket.

Negro Leagues Béisbol: A Shared Legacy

It
was
not just
about the money,
dark men—like grandpa Satch—
remained excluded from Major League play and walked
out of towns, heads bowed, backs bent, voices softened; oak-tree men
feared dusk,
feared Whites yet stood tall,
proud and free,
in the
island
sun.

Baseball as Propaganda, or The Reelection Campaign of President Trujillo,
"Long Live the Benefactor of Our Fatherland."

Fanfare for the masses, for those against
or for the regime, for those rising
out of poverty, those hoping to.
A Dragon's win will prove the nation's might,
will prove only this at-bat matters.
A Dragon's victory is a victory for peace
and prosperity. Vote Trujillo and everyone wins!

At the Stadium

Weekends too, with the summer sun intent
on ridding the island of its voice,
crowds sat on rusty bleachers, some boys
atop the outfield wall, while merengue
sounds, conjurers, and other acts entertained them.
People wiped their brows, held their breath,
didn't hold back a single scream.

The Ace Pitcher
for the Negro Leagues Baseball Museum in Kansas City, Missouri

Here is Satchel up on the mound.

Here is *a fastball wrapped in a riddle.*
Here is a batter whose heart has whittled.

Here is Ol' Satch, tree-like and wry.
Here are his arms, deceptive yet spry,
Here's his *left foot clouding the sky—.*

Here is another swinging at shadows.
Here are more pitches darting like arrows.
Here are the outfielders playing real shallow.
Here is a team condemned to the gallows.

Here is a drink, a hero's embrace.
Here is the bar, his fans, at Third Base.
Here are more tales of his feats on the plates.
Here is a stick for the bat to replace.
Here are some bottle caps to swat at and chase.

Here's to bones, to boxin', to women.
Here's to nohow, not foolin', and gittin'.
Here's to barnstormin', shadowball, and crowin'.
Here's to dirt-poor beginnings and overcomin'.
Here's to every story having multiple versions.
Here's to his fastball or his arm that you catchin'.

Hear that ole spiritual he heard through the violence.
Here is a caricature with staunch self-reliance.
Here's an American, who escaped to the islands,
whose skin found equality, though ruling the diamond.
Here is a monarch whose flight can't be silenced.

Here is proof that Negroes can bring in the crowds,
that fast and aggressive play drives the fans wild.
Here is proof that the talent the leagues had compiled
led to their ruins, once one was allowed.

Here is the hoopla and grace that created his lore.
Here is the asterisk they dangle beside all his scores.
Here is the front, though ushered in through back doors.

Here is his style, his smile, his quick wit.
Here is his uniform, his baseball, his mitt.

Here is Satchel up on the mound.

Homerun Plate a la Joshua
for Joshua Gibson

When Mami prepares this meal for you,
these simmered red kidney beans
with white rice y con concón and places
the crusty, tasty film from the bottom del caldero

onto your plate; when she dips and redips
the spoon into the thick creamy liquid to color
and flavor each bite, the nutty caramel
richness and your lips, still islands apart;

when she pierces the stuffed turkey thigh with her fork
and the juices run clear, not pink and she holds
the thickest portion of meat steady with her hands,
cuts through the joints, pulls legs from the carcass,

and says, "Uncle Josh was a mule of a man—
dark meat and intense," she means eat
your veggies too, before you can go out
and play baseball with your friends.

Satchel's Merengue Lessons and Other Shenanigans

Some games Grandpa Satch would play drunk,
mouth loose, body limber on the field.
Could be, between stripteases, the cabaret girls
taught him the island's music;
could be, he learned the natural fall
of the hip, the dance's sway and
rhythms, and worked it into every pitch.

Black Magic

He wore all white, like a Santero,
drove to the slums of Gualey or
Villa Mella, to meet a voodoo priest
and snag a wanga doll infused with
the spirit of an African god. "Anythin'
for a win." Grandpa Satch didn't know
the priest rooted for the other team.

Pregame Ritual from a Dominican Jail

After another night of jazz,
boleros and merengues, Leroy,

Cool Papa, Josh and Huesito shadowbox
drunkenly upon the first cockcrow.

Echoes of their clambake at Club V
fade with the early morning mangú,

gales of laughter and impromptu bout.
Hens cackle and newly arrived soldiers

inform Satchel, he and the others will rest or
jawbone in jail; listen to the Count, Q,

King or Ella; either way their tenantship
lessens the chances the Ciudad Trujillo

members will lose. "Take the advice and win,"
needled Ol' Satch, as he massaged his arm,

oiled it and pondered the firing squad that shall
perform its duty. So he rehearsed his playbook,

quickly recalled his pitches: the Sloppy J,
Ragtime Two-Step, the Mussolini

Slider, Midnight Rider, the Hesitation Pitch,
the infield plays and bunting scenarios. A bug

upended then crawled atop his glove. The whiff of
vintage leather, softened and worn, reminded Satch of home,

white women and the Scottsboro Boys; of how the word "rape" led
x number of lynch mobs to form and of how panic

yields a certain kind of frenzy, enough to make his old frame lob
zooming fastballs never before seen on the island of Hispaniola.

An Epic Standoff

before the threat and dismal cold
patching pieces of sky
bright waves splash
in echoes of their bombs

while fifty thousand heads swing and cry
up from the rocks to refresh us
the wind that sings

it was not dark at first the song
that opening on to the red sea humming
him two hows of a hen

no i did not want to write this
country boy Satchel showed
no and let it go

give me them back
and he kicked
as they were instead

into his windup
and he went
their own eyes

howling like owls
in the dead dark
in the throats of all men

death i know too many dead
give me his browning bark
the green grass his fastball

cautiously moving
toward the sun
guards armed with threats
it was the dragon's final stumbling-block

After a Triumphant Series

The story goes...Satch and them left
that night, with help from the American
consul, or they blowed out the next
morning, or two days later by boat—
celebrated by thousands—or by steamer, or
in September, or August, either way professional
baseball was bankrupted there for fourteen years.

Leroy "Satchel" Paige: Baseball Player

Mobile, Alabama
The Mobile Tigers
Chatanooga Black Lookouts
Birmingham Black Barons
Leopardos de Santa Clara, Cuba
Baltimore Black Sox

Cleveland Cubs
Philadelphia Giants
Wilson's Elite Giants
Pittsburgh Crawfords
Bismarck Churchills
Los Dragones de Licey, Republica Dominicana

Trujillo Stars
Newark Eagles
Club Agrario de Ciudad México
Satchel Paige's All-Stars
Kansas City Monarchs
Los Brujos de Guayama, Puerto Rico

New York Black Yankees
Memphis Red Sox
Baltimore Elite Giants
Kansas City Royals
Philadelphia Stars
Cangrejeros de Santurce, Puerto Rico

Cleveland Indians
St. Louis Barons
Chicago American Giants
Kansas City Athletics
Indianapolis Clowns
The Atlanta Braves

The National Baseball Hall of Fame in Cooperstown, New York, the "Negro Wing"
Forest Hill Memorial Park Cemetery, Kansas City, Missouri

II.

"It is now a generally accepted truth that the Trujillo Era converted the Dominican nation into a kind of chamber of psychological tortures, as well as physical and spiritual horror."
— Alan Cambeira

"But even if things were peaceful, I still would have left my country."
— Edwidge Danticat

Dim·i·nu·tion

Like rats
colonized
& plagued
we run

Whiskers
whisk rapidly
brush against
the bushes

against
the tree bark
like termites
in a spherical nest

—within
the wood—
made of mud
saliva & shit

we run
Like rats
Run bodies parallel
to ground

to roots
absorb the water
inhale the crown's
oxygen Like rats

we run
We run
like Trujillo ran
for public office

between
& behind
the bullet
& the rope

We run
like the Marines
ran drills
into Dominican

muscle memory
This is my rifle
there are many
like it but this one

is mine. We run
like the French
& the Spaniards
ran the island

—divided—
we run
We run
like borders

veils
not many
people
can wear

We run
like machetes
hold the weapon
loosely

between
the thumb
& forefinger
snap it forward

focus
on speed
like Olympic sprinters
like Jesse Owens
we run

Run that blade
through the air
aim the apex
at the macho

split it open
like coconuts
break through
the husk

slice
into
the worthless
skin

down
to the tender
flesh
We run

Like
something
meant
for field work

Something
less than
human
we run

We run
like fingers move
through rosaries
intent on prayers

we run
like elk
from black bears
we run

like foxes
from coyotes
run like
tarantulas

from spider-wasps
We run past
these woods
past the swamp

past the fire
& smoke
& scent of
burning bodies

past the screams
the metal
clinks
& clunks

the proof
of broken language
lying prostrate
past the sugarcane

we run
like cheetahs
like Model Ts
like Chevy Packards

like mustangs
like jaguars
We run like
we run past

past el río Dajabón
to the Tetelo Vargas
Stadium in San Pedro
de Macorís

past the dugouts
once filled
with Negro Leaguers
& ready rifles

& shouting fans
past the bleachers
the pitcher's mound
the diamond & the dirt

We run
past the bases
stealing glimpses
of home

We run
like "Cool
Papa" Bell
We run like light

towards
a long-enough neck
a short-enough
mouth

We run
faster than light
toward
a more flexible tongue

to push
our stories
from lungs
to larynx

to lips
We run
we run
we run

like light
past the silence.

Coffin Birth

Cento poem written mostly using lines from *The Farming of Bones* by Edwidge Danticat

She fell, making of the earth a warm bed.

Her skin, a deep bronze, between the colors of nut shells
and black salsify. The mountain dirt clung to her dress,

her arms, her face; her whole body gathering a thick cover of dust.
There were always rumors, rumors of war, of land disputes,

of one side of the island planning to invade the other.
She heard the rumors and waited for things to go from talk

to those runaway machetes in the fields.
There was the cane to curse, the harvest to dread,

the future to fear. The air, heavy with lemongrass
and flame trees losing their morning dew to the sun with the smell of all the bloc

Bound as we are to the places where our dead are lain,
her pain became a child, covered with leaf and mud stains.

Now, her flesh was simply a map of scars and bruises, a marred testament
to the tangled language of those who always stuttered as they spoke,

caught as they were on the narrow bridge between two native tongues.
The bacteria in her decomposing corpse caused the body to bloat,

her eyes to bulge out of their sockets, the tongue to swell;
it also created enough pressure to expel the fetus from her womb.

The umbilical cord had curled itself in a bloody wreath around its neck,
encircling every inch between its chin and shoulders.

A few ants crawled over its scalp, hid in the short tresses of its hair.
Look at its perfect little face, its perfect little shape, his perfect little body,

a boy child, with deep black skin, all the shades of black in it. I touch him
like one brush of a single feather, perhaps, fearing, too, that I might vanish

and wait for him to pierce the silence with his voice;
one voice like a thousand glasses breaking,

instead of the regular loud morning chatter.
There was only the sound of hummingbirds chirping,

the water gurgling, circling around all the bodies
crammed into its path. I wish at least that he were part of the air

on this side of the river, a tiny morsel in the breeze
that passes through my room in the night.

I wish at least that some of the dust of his bones
could trail me in the wind.

Conversations About the Pitfalls of the Trujillo Regime: Circa 1937

Morir Soñando

The art is in the squeeze:
in the pushing & pressing
of palm & tabletop;
in the rolling & pounding

of lemon on floor or wall.
Tío Eliezer said this
to all us children. We watched
as Tío mixed milk & sugar—

introducing spoon to mouth,
tongue to drink. Nostrils clenched,
lips pursed. Repeating the process
until raising the corners of his lips

into a neat grin. We waited
seasons for moments of beverage
& bonding. We mimicked man
while vaguely aware of the meaning.

Sometimes I turned the crank,
sharp wheel cut into metal lids.
Tío added evaporated milk,
2 cups of lemon juice & vanilla extract,

then served it
over crushed ice.
Now,
as a father,

I know the secret lies
in a relaxed & stable grip,
to keep the thumb powerful
& the hand soft, wrap fingers

around the handle
—as if a bow—
& in the continuous stirring
of sour with sweet.

The Only Thing I Have
> for my grandfather José Francisco

And this is how I remember him:
with a business card plus two pictures,
which I place side by side, next to my own;

slick black hair, mine curls into question marks.
Thick, full eyebrows, a rounded chin like lemon rind;
lips like cracks creeping into the wall of his mouth,

and a suggested smile, also like mine
—through eyes dizzied with love
and imperfections.

> The similarities melt into something
> undiscovered, unknown.

The card: Mecánico Perito en Reparaciones
de Maquinas de Coser, indicates a life seasoned
by levers, foot controls and the wild buzz

of needles. The work is guaranteed, unlike the card.
It will never guess it is a broken promise.
It will never know

> it is the only thing I have that he has touched.

Sténio Vincent's Expected Response to the Parsley Massacre, Circa 1938

Arm
yourselves
with arroz.
Believe each grain
a bullet. Cry citizenship is
my birthright. Crucifix Dominican soldiers,
show them you too can exterminate a people.
Create shivs from glass shards; burn the dead, burn the wounded. Evade
capture. Make them all remember Haitians are also human;
jostle yourselves from your apathy.
Shouldn't death always
come hard-fought,
earned?

God and Trujillo

Translated excerpts of a speech read by Dr. Joaquín Balaguer

The most trivial analysis of the national history reveals, therefore, that only as of 1930, that is, after four hundred and thirty-eight years following the Discovery, is when the Dominican people stopped being assisted exclusively by God, to be equally served by a hand that seems touched since the beginning, by a species of divine predestination:
the providential hand of Trujillo.

[...]

From that decade until present day, in a period of twenty-four years in which the stupor of the tale appears overcome by the glare of the objective reality, the man struggles with adversity and performs miracles as mighty as those achieved during the previous four centuries of the country's life by the mere effect of supernatural powers. God and Trujillo: Hereby, then, in summary, is the explanation, first, of the country's survival,
and second, of the current prosperity of Dominican life.

The Psychology of Torture

Excerpts from an interview with Rafael (Fafa) Tavares, Torture Survivor of La Cuarenta Prison, Dominican Republic

I wouldn't make contact with the base, with the ground. If they let me, I'd raise my feet. And if you don't make contact, you don't feel...the electricity [inaudible] and it came as a real surprise to them to use the charge and not have me react upon its effect. "Oh, but this son-of-a-bitch doesn't understand; he's not reacting. Fetch me the cattle prod." So the prod is..., it was..., an unfathomable experience, unbelievable—on the testicles, on top of the heart, in the eyes, in the ears, in the nose—it was a fucking unforgettable experience.

[...]

After being tortured, everyone wounded, putrid, with that feel of uncertainty in the air and the [inaudible] of the people crammed in there, you hear the night sounds: the door closing, running, the cell door locking, it was to ingrain—amongst all of those fucked and naked prisoners that were there—the idea, "Who are they coming to get?"

Michel Martelly's Expected Response to the Dominican Republic's New Migrant Rules, or How to Make a Butterfly Garden
for Haiti

Aerate the soil with your machetes,
plant coneflower and catnip, clover and violet.
Create enough space to host hiding spots;

wish each egg into a soldier,
each leaf into a platoon,
each bush a battalion.

Teach them the art of camouflage,
to shift their shape into leaf or twig,
and only feed at night, same as caterpillars.

Instruct them to sharpen their weapons,
aim their blades toward the aorta,
make the enemy's blood drench the earth.

Let them evolve into cocoon, to pupa,
to chrysalis, to sisters, to revolutionaries,
to rise as the spirits of dead warriors in disguise;

to rise as farfalla, mariposa, farasha, babochk,
paruparo, schmetterling, vlinder, borboleta,
kelebek, rama-rama, papiyon, papiyon, papiyon.

Opposing the Regime

Excerpt from an interview with Tomasina Cabral, Torture Survivor of La Cuarenta Prison, Dominican Republic

And at one in the morning...like beasts, like what they were, breaking down the door of the house [...] they entered like dogs when the owner opened the door—and they came into the bedroom, threw everything on the ground and asked me where the bombs were. I tell them, I don't have bombs. "You're coming with us!" They ransacked everything. Everything. Everything, everything. They wanted to take me in pajamas, I told them, "No. I am getting dressed."

[...]

At that moment General Tunti Sánchez yanked my hair—right there in the reception hall—[inaudible words] and he tells me to talk, because if I don't talk, those thousand men that were there would rape me. He said it using more vulgar terms that I am not going to repeat.

[...]

They began to interrogate me; they wanted to know what I knew. I told them, "No. I don't know of any bombs." Someone urged me to talk, that they already knew everything, and so, since they insisted I talk, they told me to take off my clothes, I told them, "No."

Candito Torres made it his duty to tear my clothes and strip me naked. He personally poked me with the electric cattle prod, which is a stick used to force cattle to walk into the corral. Um, in the, he struck me in the breasts, my womb, but when they realized they weren't going to get anything else, then, um, they let me be.

I got dressed with whatever I had left.

We Seek Asylum

We seek asylum from our memories, call them our country.
We, destined to exist in a spirit
of exile; we, body politic, we Dominicans
should've favored destroying Trujillo—
split apart his flesh, splintered his bones
—and made ourselves and that bastard father

holy. My own, would, as consequence, father
nine offspring; half would eventually flee the country.
The liquor, a sort of marrow for his bones,
killed him in stages. The spirits
swallowed his voice whole, unlike Trujillo,
who shouted our mob island into a republic. Dominicans

know this part of the story is true; Dominicans
also know what's been lost with our father.
How can I be a man with a father like Trujillo?
In New York, having scrubbed away the country,
a gypsy woman tells me the owl is my spirit
animal, intimately connected with the night and the moon. Bones

and bodies have been buried under this moon, under more bones,
under more bodies, many thrown into the sea. Spirit,
why is the Bachata the strangled moan of Dominicans?
Why when I say dictator do I mean empty, when I say father,
am I a guitar string, plucked and pulled deep into the backcountry
of a song whose refrain remains, "God and Trujillo"?

God and Trujillo! God, our father, who art...dead...my father. Trujillo,
remember rubbing hot sauce around my cheekbones,
your fingers, small colonies, loyal to the mother-country
of your hand; each digit a shotgun pellet spreading through this Dominican
throat, this tongue, still too young for pussy or to use the word "fuck."
The Father, as the story goes, remembers me in front of the church needing to s

off to go "fuck a girl;" remembers how low his spirit
felt and reported the incident. Trujillo,
fucked two nations, taught us to hate our blackness. My birth-father
fucked his children with his absence and his presence. Tell me, how do I debon

these memories, how do I take the blade to each Dominican
accent, cut between muscle fibers and our country?

How do I scrape off my Dominican father's spirit,
reclaim my country? Should I spit on Trujillo's
bones? Will that make me a man, will that make me?

III.

"Si alguien quiere saber cual es mi patria, no la busque, no pregunte por ella."
—Pedro Mir

"Baseball is fathers and sons playing catch, lazy and murderous, wild and controlled, the profound archaic song of birth, growth, age, and death. This diamond encircles what we are. "
—Donald Hall

1957 Sky Blue Chevrolet Packard, or The Assassination of a Dictator

I.

The bullets thunder into the dead air, the muzzle flash etches the night sky. The projectiles pierce steel frame and tinted windows & Trujillo's flesh & Trujillo's flesh & Trujillo's flesh. Traces of sulfur stagger in the breeze: everything a fractured echo.

II.

The Packard remembers last prayers & what the tortured truly clung to. What did they truly cling to?

III.

It stole so many things.

IV.

The blood in the backseat is my birth-father's; the floorboard, his torso; the seatbelts, his dangling limbs.

V.

The Packard is Anubis, it ushers souls between the world of the living & the dead.

VI.

The Packard is not death itself, not the deafening screech of ten thousand owls, not the percussive flutter of a cluster of butterflies.

VII.

Birth a billion suns or stars, rid the world of its blackness, fill ignorant life into it, curse your impure blood for being a part of the dark, paint it parsley-green.

VIII.

The San Zenon Hurricane that destroyed Santo Domingo was created by the Packard's backfire; the system of clouds & wind, bent currents & surface waves, thunderstorms & dark, funnel-shaped clouds, heavy rainfall & floods, debris & downed trees, crop damage & casualties, was fed by the exhaust pipe's heat.

IX.

The Packard prays a Rosary, each lip movement a machete slice that vibrates in accordance with the father tongue.

X.

The Packard collapses on the gravel road, surrounded by shell casings that fragmented, expanded, & even tumbled onto the stones & sand.

XI.

The humidity & high salt content of the sea air cultivates the continued corrosion of iron.

COUNSEL OF STATE
In the Name of the Republic

NUMBER 5880

CONSIDERING, that during the entire nefarious period of tyranny by the Trujillos, the most basic rights of the human person have been violated;

CONSIDERING, that the Dominican people, upon freeing themselves of that bloody tyranny, have the legitimate right to defend and preserve the state of liberty and dignity they enjoy, from the refuse and mournful relic of the past, that may conspire against their peace;

CONSIDERING, that any act or manifestation tending to evoke, exalt, in whatever form, that tyranny's shameful and unspeakable past, would and should consider themselves as a contributor or participant in stimulating the ombudsmen of said tyranny, by promoting through subversive means the return of that tyrannical and despotic regimen in conflict with the democratic system that the Dominican people now experience;

CONSIDERING, that it is the duty of the legislate, with the sense of eliminating, from the national environment those dangerous and uncivil acts that upset the public and, in addition, breed confusion in the minds of the children and the young;

HAS PRODUCED THE FOLLOWING LAW:

Article 1.— All persons who praise or exalt the Trujillo family or its tyrannical regime, aloud, or by way of screams, speeches, public or epistolary writing, printed, recorded, paintings or emblems shall be considered and judged as author of a crime against the peace and the public security and shall be punished with ten days up to a year of imprisonment or a fine of five hundred gold pesos or with both penalties at once.

Paragraph.— The same penalties will be incurred by those forming groups or meetings for the above purposes of circulating rumors about the possible restoration of the Trujillo regime, by being in conflict with the democratic system established by the Constitution of the Republic.

GIVEN by the Counsel of State, in the National Palace, Santo Domingo, National District, Capital of the Dominican Republic, on the third day on the month of May of nineteen hundred sixty-two, 119 years since the Independence and 99 since the Restoration.

RAFAEL F. BONNELLY
President of the Republic
and of the Counsel of State

Donald J. Reid Cabral,   Nicolás Pichardo,
Second Vice President   First Vice President

Luis Amiama Tió,   Monsignor Eliseo Pérez
Sánchez,
Member
Member

José Fernández Caminero,   Antonio Imbert Barrera, Member

Rafael F. Bonnelly,
President of the Dominican Republic

In exercising the powers conferred upon me by article 118 (transitory) of the Constitution of the Republic;

I PROMULGATE the following law, and declare it be published in the Official Gazette and in the newspaper *La Nación* for its disclosure and compliance.

GIVEN by the Counsel of State, in the National Palace, Santo Domingo, National District, Capital of the Dominican Republic, on the third day on the month of May of nineteen hundred sixty-two, 119 years since the Independence and 99 since the Restoration.

RAFAEL F. BONNELLY

But He Kept Law and Order

Excerpt from former Consul General to the Dominican Republic, Henry Dearborn's interview with Charles Stuart Kennedy of The Association for Diplomatic Studies and Training, Foreign Affairs Oral History Project

Initial interview date: ████████

Q: ███

DEARBORN: ███████████████████████████ the United States didn't exactly approve of him ████████████████

██

███ He had his torture chambers, ████ his political assassinations and he forced people to do things they didn't want to do.█████

██

The ████ three main props that held Trujillo in power: ████ the US, ████ the Catholic church, █████████████████

█████████ the business community ████████

██

██

People were disappearing. People were afraid to talk anywhere where people could listen to them. ███ ███ ███ ███ do not say █ anything against the government.

Lifting the Veil

The campesinos lived every line they sang in their bachatas,
shared heartaches in bars and brothels with the bachatas.

Pasarán más de mil años corazón, and they'd
still be lost, dumbfounded, in their bachata.

Ay, mami, yo no tengo culpa no, mi corazón
fue el que se enamoró, says one bachata.

Dim lights in a tiny impregnated room filled with acoustics
conjured to challenge the decency, fucking bachata?

Auto-victimization narrative, seeking solace
in a bottle of rum, a dark corner, bastard bachata.

If this was another kind of story, I'd tell you about the sea,
not rap with you about the history of the bachata.

If the bachateros were truly penitent, they'd wash dishes,
or play their woman's clitoris, not a bachata.

Lead guitar picks rather than strums, while the voice,
the timbre and texture, plead, exhort, despair. Ay bachata.

Mostly heard in the colmados or slum gatherings—treated
as backwards and vulgar—broke dick, ass out bachata.

Un hombre comiendo mango
chupándole la semilla; la creta, que bachata!

Scrape the guira, bang the bongos; double entendres
& misogyny flow heavy, dirty bachata.

During the Trujillato words worked differently, silence
equaled safety. Trujillo is dead; let's dance a bachata.

Tia Licha's House

What I remember? At four years of age
Tía Licha told me to stop —
white sheets, yellow stains.

At twelve, opening iron gates, hand in hand
Tía, rubbing index finger on my palm
saying, "This is how you get a girl to sleep with you."

Tía's house invokes memories of cherry scents,
of extreme heat, mosquito nets, outdoor latrines,
nighttime bed pans, and of containers filled with cutting water.

Who says that something dirty can't be beautiful?
Who says dirty thoughts can't be innocent?

The pipes run water. Electricity lasts
twenty hours or more. She has a kitten now,
and most days there's food enough for two.

Fetching Water

The house in Los Jardines where my birth-father lived with his third wife
and my half-brother and sister, had a patio, the patio a tile floor,

the floor a cedar rocker and a window, the rocker by the window,
Keiter in plain sight. My eyes, lost ships at sea. I was ten.

Raindrops thrashed metal roofs and unpaved roads. When it clears,
Keiter's fingers wrap around empty gallons of water

her tiny feet slated for the watering hole.
On her return, I see the load, practically an anchor

against her frame; I see drops of sweat slide down her face:
from forehead, to nose, to cheek, then lips.

She rests a moment, as if conscious of her distant future:
a husband, two kids, and many more bone-tired days like these.

A Recipe Story

for my mother Virginia

That's Paula Deen!
Mami's lips—dark brown,
like a gumbo of greens thickened
with roux—sweeten. She returns

to the trill of stirring
and the scent of Southern
Cuisine. Thick Spanish
mimics a twangy *Hey Y'all*.

Mami replaces paprika
for comino, parsley for cilantro.
We watch her TV show,
know her sons and brother

also cook—I know her laugh.
Cornbread con canela trails
trapped in the wind.
The clouds dream of rain

or snow. I stand outside
Paula's restaurant, press
nose to glass. Mami
peels mangos, slices fruit.

Baseball/Worship

Because her prayer was answered, because I returned safely home,
because drugs and police and New York failed to swallow me whole,

my mother and I made the pilgrimage to Higüey,
to la Basilica de la Altagracia.

Hopped on a bus from la capital, drove through San Pedro de Macorís,
its endless fleet of baseball fields, its carajitos,

eating one meal a day, avoiding anything spicy,
abandoning gossip and school, clutching makeshift bats,

both hands reaching towards sky, crossing the diamond on their knees,
tasting the dirt at their throats, clawing the dirt on bare feet,

all of this an offering of sorts.

Or Simply, Just Rice

Dying of cirrhosis of the liver, fatigued, yellowed
eyes, jaundiced tongue, Papi hollered for her light,
Virginia...my scotch!!

By then Mami left him because of the drink,
left him for reasons I was too young to understand.

Yet whenever he came into town
she would cook his favorite meal.

White rice, black beans, sautéed onions, steak, a side of concón
chased with a rum and coke—beans baked overnight,
pre-soaked next to thoughts of what to wear, what make-up—

tight Sassoon jeans, white blouse, red rouged lips.
A hint of mascara highlighted tired eyes.

Be sure to add a cup and a half of water per every cup of rice.
Add two tablespoons of oil, an olive. Add a paper towel
to halo the rice; keep the moisture in.
Place the lid, reduce flame to a steam.

Place the meat on the stove, warming to room temperature.

Retrieve a glass from the cupboard, ice from the freezer,
soda from the fridge, rum from her bedroom.

Stir.

Love requires this kind of attention.

I massaged his feet at the hospice, rubbed swollen limbs,
heard my mother's name burn on his lips.

The Perfect Game

The perfect game
unlike the perfect father
is possible. The feat:

a series of solitary acts,
in which no opposing player
reaches base, where the pitcher

does not permit any balls to connect
with the meat of the bat,
nor allow walks or a hit by pitch

and is also backed with solid fielding
by the other eight players.
Groundballs stopped short at second base,

a long line drive thwarted at center field,
a sliding catch inches from first,
and the s w o o p s w o o p s w o o p

of the ball landing in the catcher's mitt. Fatherhood
too, insists on this relationship between things,
yet, it remains something some sidle over

like when superstition creeps in
after the 5th or 6th inning as teammates
isolate themselves from the pitcher,

believing the mere mention
of the undertaking affects the outcome.
There shall only be twenty-seven men up,

twenty-seven men down. Each defiantly poised
against the years, against the season, each moment like everything
between fathers and sons, between men, tender yet tense.

And He Will Play Baseball

bat lefty like Big Papi—
the bat: an extension of his arm,
a coming together of white ash,

rubber, fabric, and stitched cowhide.
I know this because he grips the ball tight,
searches for ground, breath meeting my gaze

then lets it drop from his fingers
like the dull roar of a first *I love you*.
I lower him headfirst; back slightly hollowing

arms extending forward—as if diving—
while he retrieves the ball. Barehanded.
Returning him to my shoulders,

hand supporting his bottom, the other his waist,
the ball, the raised corners of his mouth,
the squinting of the eyes, show me

this too is fatherhood;
this too will teach him
how to love a man.

For You, For Asking Me Why I Love Baseball So Much

Because baseball players are as much artists as painters or sculptors,
and yes, because everyone deserves to see great art often.

Because it is fall and the crisp night air fills with the crack of bats
and stomp of feet and grown men with guttural growls,

who chew tobacco and play a game they love. Because, really,
didn't we all pretend to make the game-winning play?

The Lorenzo Cain three-run double; or the Gordon homer, the ball
smaller and smaller in the royal-blue sky; the aggressive sprint for a run

—bold and dramatic—with Hosmer stealing home; or the Davis fastball:
inside corner, inches away from the bat, faster than a blink,

because maybe the batter blinked and only heard the thunderous swoop
of the ball landing like a meteor on Salvy's mitt.

Because baseball can be an island, can be a country, a world
and a loss is paramount to heartache or death and a rally

can be a planet discovered. A moon. Because a win can be a shutout,
can be hard-fought, can be a come-back, can be overdue.

Because a win can be a childhood dream, an answered prayer,
my father reborn: his teeth, his glass of rum, his burning throat;

or it can be my mother, her fragile hands, no discoordination
of movement, no resting tremor; one hand to support my infant neck,

the other my bottom. Cradled safely in this stadium,
as they climb steps, maneuver between aisles and peanut vendors.

Because this game can explain a life lived,
a year or six, a moment or two, this breath.

EPILOGUE

Stealing Home

You should have seen my father's arms, swinging
proudly down the street as he held his lover's hand.

You should have seen my father's hand, fingers draped,
tight, tender, around the palm, as he held that lover's hand.

You should have seen my father's face; you should have seen
my mother's face, as he cocked his lover's hand.

You should've witnessed his stance, seen him shoulder and mount the arm
like a shotgun, pull and push the weapon back, as he released his lover's hand.

You should've felt the buildings shake; you should've heard each voice
quiver then boom, like small shallow earthquakes, as he cursed his lover's hand.

You should've seen the signs crash and crumble like Trujillo's corpse,
streets screaming and crying—1961 again—as he disposed of his lover's hand.

You should've watched the Cruz de Malta scent plant itself in my mother's
memory, reminding her she is animal, as she followed his lover's hand.

You should've noticed my thrill, seen my bat and satchel fall, heard
my footsteps headed towards my father, as he imagined his lover's hand.

You should have seen his lover, rounding the corners like bases,
as my mother's name escaped his lips, as he petitioned his lover's hand.

You should've seen the ring get pitched—my mother's knuckleball—little to no sp
difficult to control or catch, as my father's story debased his lover's hand.

You should've heard the Aybar family break, seen our household split and shatte
like bones, like bats, like waves—like dawns breaking as he held his lover's hand.

NOTES

Prologue

"Remembering the Dead" contains a quote from the documentary film, *Pitchin' Man: Satchel Paige—Defying Time*, produced by Refocus Films.

Section I

"Corpse Disposal": On September 3, 1930, the category 4 San Zenon hurricane struck the island of the Dominican Republic. Newly elected into office, President Rafael L. Trujillo, with the help of the American Red Cross, was able to rebuild the city. It is rumored that, before the storm, Trujillo and his men killed many of the reported hurricane victims.

"Baseball's Traveling Men" was inspired by translation work I had performed for the Negro Leagues Baseball Museum in Kansas City, Missouri and took its shape and direction from the Espada poem. It talks about the bond and cultural exchange that occurred between African American and Latino/Caribbean players before the breaking of the color barrier.

"The Rise of a Dictator" references a newspaper article from the *BUFFALO COURIER-EXPRESS*, Sunday, Jan. 4, 1959, where Trujillo inaugurates a hospital for Dr. Miguel Brioso. It also contains the title of an online essay, "Articulatory Difficulties in the Acquisition of Spanish /r/ in a Bilingual Context" written by Manuela González-Bueno. It specifically mentions "the cutting" or the Haitian massacre, where people suspected of being Haitian were asked to pronounce the word for parsley in Spanish (perejil); those who failed to trill the r or speak the j, were killed.

"The Ace Pitcher" contains lines from the book *Satchel: The Life and Times of an American Legend* written by Larry Tye.

"Homerun Plate a la Joshua": Joshua "Josh" Gibson is considered one of the greatest catchers and best power hitters of all time. He was so great, those who saw him play consider Babe Ruth to be the white Josh Gibson. At Café Lindbergh in the Dominican Republic, both he and Satchel had dishes named after them.

"Pregame Ritual from a Dominican Jail": During that 1937 summer baseball season, Satchel along with the other Negro Leaguers are rumored to have been placed in prison to ensure they were well-rested and prepared to win their games. It takes part of its title from Dr. Martin Luther King Jr.'s "Letter from A Birmingham Jail."

"An Epic Standoff" is a cento poem using lines from the following texts: *The Tropics of Baseball*, Rob Ruck; "1919", Anonymous; "South", Kamau Brathwaite; "Stone", Kamau Brathwaite; "The Wind in the Dooryard", Derek Walcott; "Sea Canes", Derek Walcott; "The Visibility Trigger", Kamau Brathwaite; "Codicil", Derek Walcott; "Roy (for Father)", Cheryl Boyce-Taylor; "Beyond the Great Mississippi", Jordan A. Deustch; "Island in the Sun—Side 2", Kendel Hippolyte; *Tropics of Baseball*, Rob Ruck; "Folkways" (from "The Spades"), Kamau Brathwaite; "365", Jack Buck; "Casey at the Bat", Garrison Keillor; "The Reasons for Rainbows: A Song to Baseball", J. Patrick Lewis; "October", Hester Jewell Dawson; "third world views", Jean Binta Breeze.

Section II

Quotes are from the book *Quisqueya la bella: Dominican Republic in Historical and Cultural Perspective* (Routledge, 2014) and *The Farming of Bones* by Edwidge Danticat (Soho Press, 2013).

"Dim·i·nu·tion" is my take on the beginning of the Haitian Massacre, also known as the Parsley Massacre. It contains a line from Edwidge Danticat's classic novel, *The Farming of Bones* and from The Marine Corps' Rifleman Creed.

"Coffin Birth": Cento poem that is written mostly using lines from *The Farming of Bones*. Slight changes were made to some of the original lines to fit the new text. The section that describes the actual scientific phenomena is from the following link: http://health.howstuffworks.com/diseases-conditions/death-dying/dying4.htm.

"Morir Sonando" literally means to die dreaming. It is a delicious drink from the Dominican Republic very similar to an Orange Julius. My uncle prepared it with limes.

"Sténio Vincent's Expected Response to the Parsley Massacre: Circa 1938": Sténio Vincent was president of Haiti from November 18, 1930 to May 15, 1941.

"God and Trujillo": My translation of these excerpts of Balaguer's speech, who also became president of the island. Published in "Clio", *Dominican Academy of History*, Volume XXII, No. 101, October-December 1954. Read by Dr. Joaquin Balaguer on November 14, 1954. Abelardo Nanita, editor: *The Trujillo Era*, Volume I. Year of the Benefactor of the Fatherland, Dominican Printer, Ciudad Trujillo, 1955, p. 50-61.

"The Psychology of Torture" and "Opposing the Regime": I transcribed and translated these excerpts spoken by the actual torture victims. The videos can be found on YouTube, La Carcel de la 40 (parts 1, 2, and 3) presented by Un tiempo después/www.Cachicha.com.

"Michel Martelly's Expected Response to the Dominican Republic's New Migrant Rules or How to Make a Butterfly Garden": Michel Martelly was the president of Haiti since May of 2011 until stepping down early in 2016, leaving no successor. This piece also references the Mirabal Sisters who openly opposed the Trujillo dictatorship and were known as "The butterflies." The Mirabals were the inspiration for the United Nations General Assembly and the designation of the International Day for the Elimination of Violence against Women, every November 25th, the day their corpses were found.

"We Seek Asylum" contains a line from the poem "Benediction" by Chris Abani.

Section III

"Law 5880": I translated this Dominican law, which was put into effect after Trujillo's assassination.

"Lifting the Veil": Bachata's rise came a year to the date of the assassination; the music is stated to have been a way for the people to express themselves after so many years of silence. The poem contains: a quote from the History of Bachata link on the 2Step2 website; the line, "Ay, mami, yo no tengo culpa no", is from an Anthony Santos bachata; the line, "If this was another kind of story...", is from Junot Díaz's novel, *This is How You Lose Her*; the line, "Un hombre comiendo mango", is from a Luis Vargas bachata.

"The Perfect Game" was inspired by and ends with a variation on a quote from Donald Hall's essay, "Fathers Playing Catch with Sons."

"For You, For Asking Me Why I Love Baseball So Much" references the Kansas City Royals and their 2015 World Series win against the New York Mets.

Epilogue

"Stealing Home" was inspired by the essay, "It Never Rains in Tiger Stadium" by John Ed Bradley; it also begins with the same first line as Bradley's text, "You should have seen my father's arms."

About the Poet

Gustavo Adolfo Aybar is a Dominican writer, raised in New York, Los Angeles, and Miami Beach. He graduated from the University of Missouri-Kansas City where he received his MA in Romance Languages & Literature. He is a Cave Canem and Artist Inc. I/II fellow, plus a member of the Latino Writer's Collective (501c3). His work can be found in their anthology, *Primera Pagina: Poetry from the Latino Heartland.* Other publications include: *NINE: A Journal of Baseball History & Culture Volume 24-2,* and *I-70 Review* Summer 2017 issue.

His chapbook, *Between Line Breaks* was released May 2016 from Spartan Press.

Currently, Aybar is working on translating the works of Mexican author/playwright Glafira Rocha from Spanish to English. Some translations of Rocha's stories can be found in the online journals *EZRA, Asymptote* and *The Brooklyn Rail's InTranslation* where Rocha's short story "Interspersed Signs" was selected as a Pushcart nominee for Fiction in 2014.

www.ingramcontent.com/pod-product-compliance
Lightning Source LLC
Chambersburg PA
CBHW021026120726
47905CB00009B/3203